INDUSTRIAL AMERICA
1940-1960

173 Photographs by
ANDREAS FEININGER

Dover Publications, Inc.
New York

Frontispiece: Wooden oil derricks, Signal Hill Oil Field, Long Beach, California, 1947.

The photographs on the following pages were produced on assignment for LIFE Magazine, Copyright © 1940–60 by Time Inc., and are reproduced here by courtesy of Time Inc.: *frontispiece,* 3–6, 8–12, 14–24, 26–39, 41–69, 76/77, 84, 86, 89, 90, 95, 97–103, 106–109, 112–115, 117–121, 124, 125, 136, 138–177, 184/185.

Published in Canada by General Publishing Company, Ltd., 30 Lesmill Road, Don Mills, Toronto, Ontario.
Published in the United Kingdom by Constable and Company, Ltd., 10 Orange Street, London WC2H 7EG.

Industrial America, 1940–1960: 173 Photographs by Andreas Feininger is a new work, first published by Dover Publications, Inc., in 1981.

International Standard Book Number: 0-486-24198-X
Library of Congress Catalog Card Number: 81-68278

Manufactured in the United States of America
Dover Publications, Inc.
180 Varick Street
New York, N.Y. 10014

Introduction

The 173 photographs in this collection originated between 1940 and 1960, documenting a period when American industry, spurred by the war effort to unprecedented heights of productivity, expanded almost explosively. This vital and aggressive force not only sustained an ever-expanding economy and provided the material necessities indispensable to win a war, but also, because of its often dramatic manifestations, lent itself particularly well to pictorial documentation.

Although I had done a moderate amount of industrial coverage during the late Thirties, I became seriously interested in this fascinating field of photography only in 1942 when, thanks to the efforts of my friend Ewing Krainin, I was commissioned by the Office of War Information (OWI) to do a series of photo-reportages on various war industries. Some of the results of this work are the images on pages 70, 71, 73, 74, 75, 78, 79, 80, 81, 82, 83, 85, 87, 91, 92, 93, 94, 104, 105, 110, 111, 122, 123, 126, 128, 130, 131, 134, 135, 137, 178, 179, 180, 181, 182 and 183. Many of the other photographs were taken by me on a multitude of assignments for *Life*, where I was employed as a staff photographer from 1943 to 1962. I also wish to take this opportunity to express my deeply felt thanks to my publisher and friend Hayward Cirker, President of Dover Publications, Inc.; without his active interest in my work, these photographs might have stayed buried in dusty files forever.

Many of my readers will doubtless wonder why I took all my photographs in black-and-white instead of color. There are two reasons: one, because at the time most of these pictures were made, Kodachrome, then the only available color film, was still maddeningly slow; the other, because I felt I could do justice to my dramatic subjects only by translating them into powerful and "graphic" black-and-white—a medium that offers a degree of artistic control infinitely greater than that available to photographers working in color.

Actually, the vast majority of all industrial subjects is rather colorless, notwithstanding the drama and excitement aroused in the spectator by fire and smoke, the hiss of steam, the clamor of turning wheels and the whole atmosphere of frenzied activity occasionally raised to a pitch of madness. Dominating, as a rule, are black and shades of dirty gray, while pleasing colors are rare—especially in the old days before the drabness of machinery blackened by smoke and soot had given way to the relative cleanliness of electrically operated equipment painted in appealing "designer colors"—pale green, light gray or beige—accented, when needed, by the "warning colors" yellow and red. But at the time I did most of my industrial work, color was immaterial.

Whether or not an industrial photograph turns out successfully—capturing the essence of the scene or event—depends, in my opinion, primarily on the photographer's ability to "see in terms of the camera." Never must he let himself forget the fact that the eye and the camera "see" differently. The eye, subject to the selective (and visually limiting) guidance of the brain, "sees" *subjectively* and pays attention only to that in which the person is interested; the camera—a machine—"sees" *objectively*, that is, registers *everything*, no matter whether pictorially important, superfluous or visually distracting. This is the main reason why so many photographs turn out disappointingly: the photographer failed to "see" that the contrast between the lightest and darkest areas of a scene was either too high or too low to enable him to make a technically satisfactory picture; that the direction or quality of the incident light was unsuitable to the occasion; that the background was too ugly, too distracting or otherwise influenced adversely the appearance of the subject proper of the picture; and so on. If the following photographs convey something of the beauty, the power and the excitement of the industrial scene (an accomplishment that only the reader can judge), it is because never for a moment did I let myself forget the difference between human and photographic "seeing," rigorously avoiding those subjects and scenes which experience and instinct told me would yield only insipid pictures.

To readers interested in phototechnical background information, I want to say that not once did I use a 35 mm camera. Roughly half of the pictures were made with a 2¼-x-2¼-inch Rolleiflex and the other half with a 4-x-5-inch view camera, the latter, of course, permitting me to use lenses of different focal lengths and to exert perspective control. To preserve as much as possible the usually very typical (and therefore pictorially important) mood and "atmosphere" of a scene, I made all my pictures by "available light," using shadow fill-in illumination only when technical reasons demanded it. But even then I was always extremely careful not to destroy the character of the original light because it is my conviction that more than any other single factor, it is the quality and the character of the illumination that create the mood of a scene—and it is the mood that makes the difference between a "*snap*" and a *picture*.

ANDREAS FEININGER

INDUSTRIAL AMERICA
1940-1960

Mining

No industrialized nation can thrive without a flourishing mining industry which supplies it with the metals, minerals and fossil fuels indispensable to its welfare. Such activities can take three basic forms: underground mining and drilling, open-pit mining (quarrying) and strip mining.

In underground mining, a vertical shaft is sunk (or a hole drilled) into the ground until it reaches the coveted veins of metal or beds of coal or uranium, which then are excavated by way of horizontal tunnels or "drifts." If the desired minerals occur in the form of concentrated bodies of ore or industrially valuable rocks penetrating (or at least close to) the surface, huge holes are dug into the ground and the valuable deposits are excavated in open pits. In strip mining, which is used almost exclusively for the extraction of coal located at shallow depths, the "overburden"—the overlaying layers of sand, gravel or soil—is "stripped" away by means of huge machinery and deposited on dumping grounds in rows or piles called "tailings" to expose the coal, which thereby becomes accessible to surface excavating equipment.

Necessary as these operations may be, they have some very undesirable and occasionally even catastrophic effects upon the environment. Most devastating in this respect are strip mining, which turns huge areas of once life-supporting land into sterile and permanent deserts, and underground uranium mining, which leaves mountains of radioactive waste or "tailings" exposed to the elements. Wind then carries lung-cancer-causing radioactive dust over hundreds of square miles with dire consequences for any breathing creature, including man, while rain leaches out the radioactive particles, which sink into the soil, penetrate to groundwater levels and poison nearby rivers, springs and waterholes. Although some legislation exists to counteract these insidious threats to life, in actuality very little is being done while the disastrous effects grow daily.

Tailings from underground mining operations at Butte, Montana, 1944. The tall structures near the center are headframes which accommodate the shaft's elevator machinery.

Above: Mining operation at Butte, Montana, showing tailings and headframes. Butte is known as "the richest hill on earth." The famous Anaconda shaft was sunk in 1879. The Kelley shaft, opened in 1952, was 2,200 feet deep by 1954, when it produced 12,000 tons of copper ore per day. *Opposite:* A section of the Bingham copper mine, Utah, 1954. During the previous 50 years, more than a billion tons of copper ore and waste rock had been taken from this huge open-pit mine, creating a man-made canyon approximately 2,000 feet deep. At that time, the mine had produced more than a billion dollars worth of copper.

Coal

Not so long ago, coal was considered obsolescent as a source of energy. A host of smaller coal mines had to shut down as unprofitable, coal-carrying railroads were in serious financial trouble, old power plants converted from coal to oil and new ones were designed to use atomic fuel. Not so anymore. The steady rise in the cost of fuel oil suddenly made coal look good again, and today more coal is mined and burned than ever before.

Coal is obtained either through strip mining or underground mining. On the following two pages I show some of the equipment used for each type of mining as it looked some twenty-five years ago.

The gigantic piece of machinery on page 8 is a Marion shovel which strips the overburden from a coal bed that provides fuel for the Muskingum River plant, built and operated by the Ohio Power Company at Beverly, Ohio. The shovel is electrically powered and trails a monstrous cable 4½ miles long which connects it with the power plant. It stands 121 feet tall, as high as a 12-story building. Its dipper, 19 feet 7 inches deep, 13 feet across and 9 feet high, equipped with steel teeth 21 inches long and 10 inches wide, rips oaks with 12-inch trunks out of the ground as if they were weeds and can remove 2,000 cubic yards of overburden per hour. Standing with my camera in front of this rock- and tree-devouring monster, I felt like a pygmy confronting a raging dinosaur.

The Robot Miner on page 9 was photographed at the Broken Arrow Coal Company's Wellston, Ohio, mine. It was designed to work profitably very shallow coal seams which previously had to be dug unprofitably by hand. It is operated by an electronic screen which tells the operator whether the cutting head remains on the coal seam or strays into adjoining harder rock. This machine is capable of penetrating 1000 feet into the side of a hill, spewing out a steady stream of coal upon an attached conveyor belt which carries the coal directly to dump trucks waiting outside.

Opposite: Bulldozers work on the stockpile of a coal-burning steam-electric power plant.

8 A Marion strip shovel removes the overburden from a coal bed.

A Robot Miner chews its way through an underground coal seam.

Left: Coal conveyor belt at the Muskingum River power plant at Beverly, Ohio. Built in 14 sections, it is 4½ miles long, crosses the Muskingum River on a 700-foot suspension bridge, and carries coal from mine to power plant at a rate of 600 feet per minute and 800 tons per hour. *Above:* The Muskingum River power plant photographed by the light of the rising full moon.

Hydroelectric Power

A hydroelectric power plant converts the energy of falling water into electricity. The photograph on pages 14 and 15 shows Shasta Dam on the Sacramento River near Redding, California. Here is its history.

In 1954, when I took this picture, Shasta Dam was the second-largest and second-tallest concrete structure ever built by man. It towers 602 feet above bedrock (the height of a 60-story skyscraper), higher than the Washington Monument. It measures 3,500 feet across its curving crest. With appurtenant works, it contains 8,710,000 cubic yards of concrete—enough to build a three-foot-wide walkway around the world at the Equator. Water falling over the 375-foot-wide spillway in the center of the dam drops 480 feet—three times the height of Niagara Falls.

Completed by the Bureau of Reclamation in 1949, Shasta is a multipurpose dam. It impounds 4,500,000 acre-feet of water—enough to provide 1,000 gallons of water for every man, woman and child in the U.S. Its functions are to regulate the flow of the river and improve navigation, to provide irrigation and flood control, and to generate electric power. Its 375,000-kilowatt capacity is sufficient to supply all the electrical needs for a city of 500,000 people. Together with the Keswick Dam power plant, which forms the afterbay or regulating reservoir for Shasta, the total generation during 1954 was 2,714,787,800 kilowatt hours.

Energy from Shasta drives the big pumps that lift Sacramento River water uphill 200 feet into a canal to irrigate the fertile but dry San Joaquin Valley. The remainder of its output is sold to domestic, agricultural and industrial customers throughout the steadily growing northern California area.

Opposite: Arrow Rock dam, Idaho.

Shasta Dam on the Sacramento River near Redding, California. The sunken derrick at the left is a leftover from the construction of the dam, which was completed in 1949.

14

16

Above: Hoover (originally Boulder) Dam in the Black Canyon of the Colorado River on the Arizona–Nevada boundary line. Built by the Bureau of Reclamation and completed in 1936, it was the highest dam in the world when I photographed it in 1948—726 feet above bedrock, as tall as a 72-story skyscraper. In the foreground and to the right are the waters of Lake Mead, the 115-mile-long reservoir created by the dam. *Opposite:* The view from the crest of Hoover Dam looking south, with Arizona on the left side and Nevada on the right side of the river.

Hoover Dam power-transmission lines. The hollow cables are almost 1½ inches in diameter and carry 287,000 volts to Los Angeles. Spans are up to 1,000 feet between towers. In 1954,

the country's electric-power consumption was approximately 471,609,103,000 kilowatt hours; of this, hydroelectric plants generated 107,130,521,000 kilowatt-hours or 22.7 percent of the total.

19

Opposite: 10,000-horsepower electric motor for an oil tanker, photographed at the General Electric plant in Schenectady some 30 years ago. At that time, electric motors provided approximately 85 percent of all the power used in American factories, and scientists had calculated that the electric power used in industry gave every American worker the equivalent of 236 strong men to help him on his job—more than twice the help given to European workers at that time. *Above:* The huge shaft of a dynamo being finished at General Electric's Schenectady plant. In the early Fifties, approximately 100,000 different kinds of electric motors were in production, from minute 0.002-horsepower motors used in bomber defense systems to gigantic 65,000-horsepower motors for dam pumps.

Above: This picture of the cyclotron at the University of California, one of the basic instruments used in nuclear research, was taken around 1950. Compared to modern particle accelerators, what then was a giant is now a dwarf. *Opposite:* High-voltage research lab equipment, photographed in 1949. Its enormous size becomes apparent when one compares it with the tiny figure of the man in the bosun's chair at the top of the picture.

Oil

By mid-1980, probably the most crucial and critical of all raw materials was oil, then priced at over $32.00 per barrel for Middle East crude. In the early Fifties, when the following pictures were taken, matters were very different; oil was plentiful and sold for an average of $2.76 per barrel for domestic crude of 27° gravity. Following is some additional information that might have historical interest.

In 1954, capital expenditures for the oil industry were over $4 billion 600 million —a record. Drilling activity, too, set a new record with some 53,000 wells completed, an increase of 3,500 over the preceding year. Of these, however, more than one-third were dry holes. Domestic demand for oil was estimated at 2 billion 824 million barrels, up 39 million barrels over 1953. Natural-gas output for 1954 was 11 trillion cubic feet, an increase of more than 368 billion cubic feet over 1953. At that time, the oil industry accounted for approximately 2,400 primary products including waxes; in addition, by-products were innumerable.

The Signal Hill oil field near Long Beach, California, which is depicted on pages 26–33, was "discovered" on June 25, 1921. Between that time and January 1954, some 1,300 wells had been drilled in the field. The deepest well on record (approximately three miles deep) was drilled in 1938 by the Shell Oil Company and proved to be dry. The deepest producing zone was some 10,300 feet below the surface, a depth of approximately two miles. In 1954, the field's annual production was about 7,400,000 barrels, representing, at that time, a value of approximately $19 million per year.

Today's oil fields look very different from Signal Hill in the Fifties. Derricks are of steel instead of wood and are taken down as soon as the well is producing instead of being left in place as previously was the custom. This makes for less dramatic scenery and takes away some of the romance of the struggle for oil but saves on cost and leaves a cleaner view.

Opposite: An oil tank in Louisiana—symbol of prosperity and wealth.

Signal Hill oil field, Long Beach, California, as it appeared in 1947. Instead of trees, derricks. Temporary oil-storage tanks mingle with shoddy buildings. The acrid stench of crude oil is everywhere. *Overleaf:* Highway crossing Signal Hill oil field, photographed 1947. *Pages 30–33:* Signal Hill oil field as it appeared in the Forties. *Pages 34–37:* The Baton Rouge refinery of the Esso Standard Oil Company of Louisiana. During the years 1952–54, this plant processed an average of 250,000 barrels of crude oil daily. In addition to motor gasoline, it also produced from oil other chemicals as well as material for aviation gasoline and synthetic rubber. According to the Standard Oil Company, at that time the Baton Rouge refinery was the largest in the U.S. and one of the largest in the world, although a refinery at Aruba had a larger processing capacity and the one at Abadan had a larger capacity at the time it was shut down.

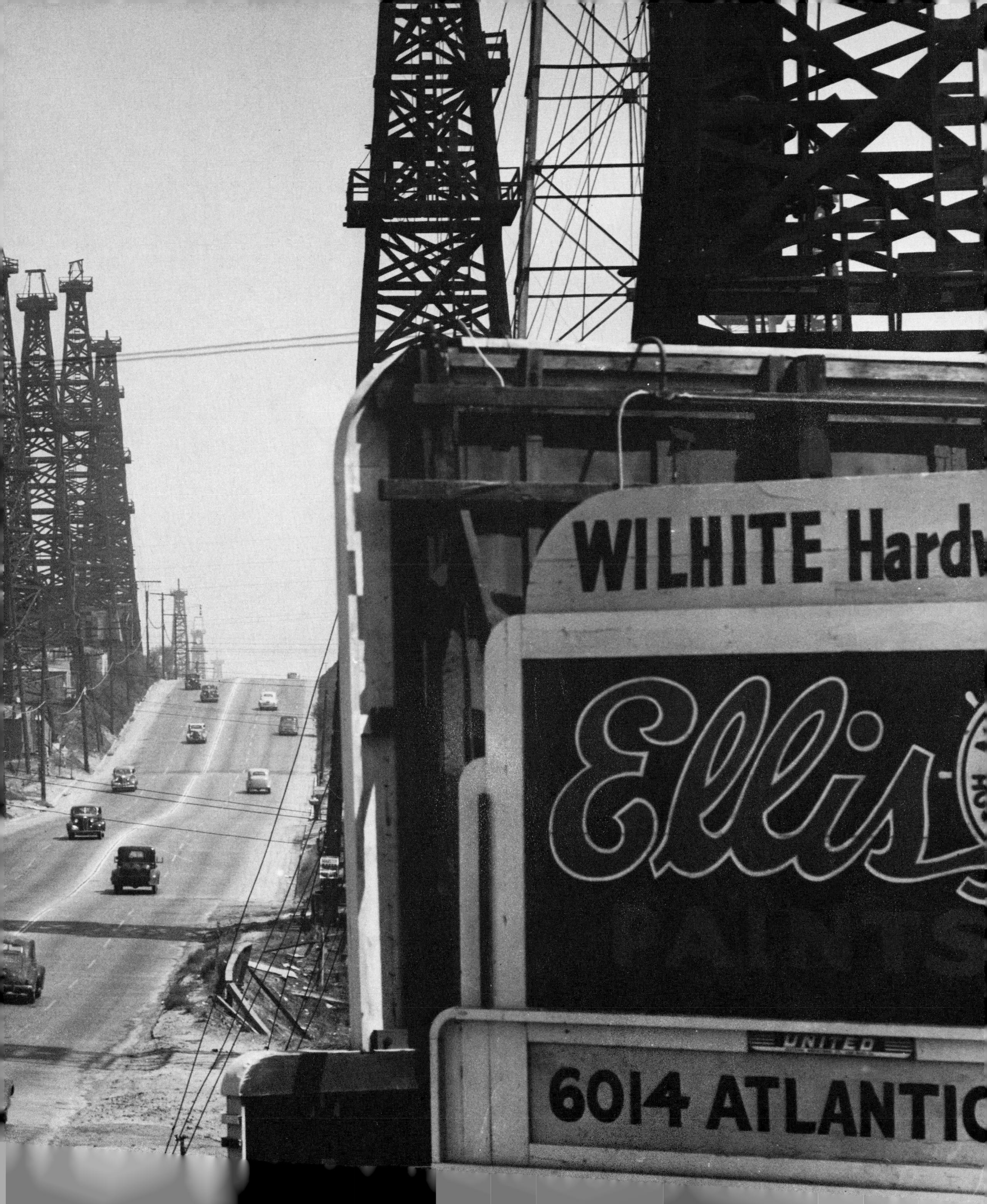
WILHITE Hardw
Ellis
UNITED
6014 ATLANTIC

Butadiene plant near Houston, Texas. Butadiene, derived from butane, is a colorless, odorless gas, easily liquified and highly inflammable. It is used in the manufacture of synthetic rubber.

Steel

All the photographs documenting steel production on pages 41–67 were made in 1944 at various plants of the U.S. Steel Corporation.

The chief raw materials of steel are iron ore, coal (coke) and limestone. Steel production starts by smelting iron ore in a blast furnace fueled by coke, which also acts as the reducing agent. Limestone provides the base for slag, which fluxes away the nonmetallic impurities inherent in ore and coke. At regular intervals, the blast furnace is tapped and the molten iron is transferred via huge ladles either to the "mixer," where it is kept molten until it goes to the steel-making furnace, or to the pig-casting machine, where it is cast into "pigs," bars of raw iron weighing from 50 to 100 pounds.

Iron is transformed into steel by one of three kinds of furnaces: the Bessemer converter, the open hearth or the electric furnace. During the melting process, careful checks on fuel input, temperature and slag conditions, as well as the addition of specific amounts of ferric oxide and ferromanganese, are required to achieve the desired composition and quality of the molten mass of steel called a "heat."

When, after 10 to 12 hours in the blast furnace, the "heat" is finished, the furnace is tapped and the molten steel drained into a giant ladle capable of holding up to 200 tons of liquid steel. An overhead crane lifts the filled ladle and carries it to the pouring platform where flatbed cars loaded with ingot molds await the metal, which is poured into these forms; this operation is called "teeming." The size of the ingot molds depends upon the desired size of the ingots, which in turn depends upon the kind of mill required to make the finished product. Weight of the ingots usually varies between 5,000 and 40,000 pounds but may run as high as 200,000 pounds.

After being stripped from the mold, the red-hot ingots are transferred to the gas-heated soaking pit where they stay until they are of uniform rolling temperature; from there they go to the respective rolling mill where they are transformed into the final product: structural steel, rails, heavy plate or sheet metal.

Opposite: "Teeming"—pouring molten steel from a ladle into ingot molds.

U.S. Steel's Edgar Thompson mill, Pittsburgh, Pa. The two complex structures in the center are blast furnaces. In the foreground, workers cross a railroad overpass on their way home. A perpetual acrid haze used to veil this huge industrial complex.

42

44

Columbia-Geneva Steel Division, U.S. Steel Corporation, near Provo, Utah. Using Utah ore and Utah coal, this is a fully integrated and

self-sufficient plant. Blast furnaces are in the center, open-hearth furnaces at the right. In the background is snow-covered Mt. Timpanogos.

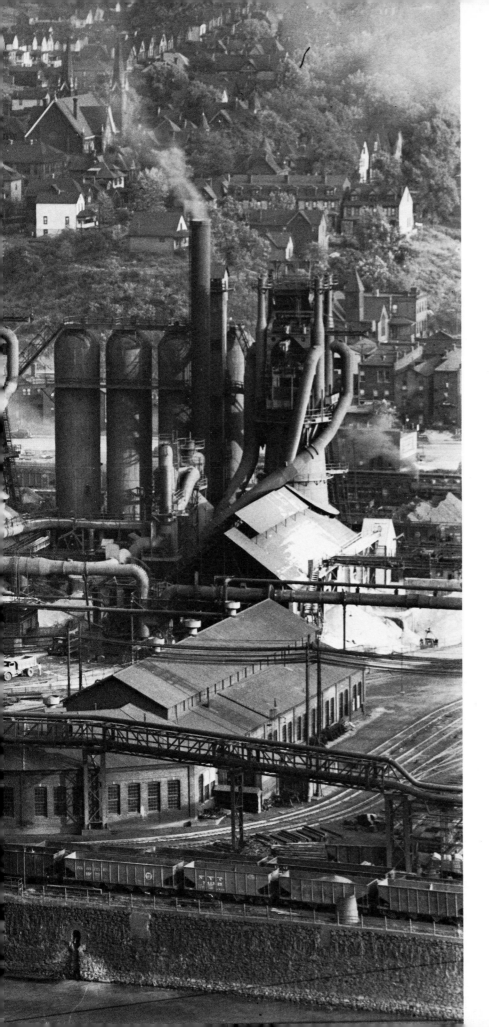

A typical "old-fashioned" steel mill in a Pennsylvania valley. In the foreground are a river (for cooling-water and to accommodate barges loaded with supplies) and a freight train loaded with coal. Open-hearth furnaces at the left are easily recognized by the cluster of tall chimneys. Three blast furnaces in the background together with their stoves (the tall cylindrical vessels) supply the heated air which is forced through the "burden" materials in the furnace to properly melt the "heat."

Silhouettes of blast furnaces at sunset, a symbol of industrial might.

Above: A closer look at the three blast furnaces of U.S. Steel's Edgar Thompson mill—a functional tangle of steel. *Opposite:* At the left side, a row of open-hearth furnaces; at the right, ingots being filled with molten steel.

Tapping an open-hearth furnace. The molten steel, heavier than slag, flows first, nearly filling the ladle. The slag, which follows, overflows the ladle and is caught in the adjoining slag thimble.

"Teeming." Across the way from the row of open-hearth furnaces
is the pouring platform, where ingot molds are successively filled
with molten steel by lifting a stopper in the bottom of the ladle.

Bessemers in a U.S. Steel plant. *Above:* Control room. *Opposite:* Bessemers "blowing." This is a spectacular sight. At night, when the Bessemers blow, the sky lights up for miles with a fiery glow.

Blooming mill. *Above:* An ingot is rolled into a "bloom," the semifinished material for structural beams, rails, axles, etc. Rolled back and forth in a reversing stand, the dimensions of the bloom are reduced with each pass as it becomes longer and longer while a manipulator turns it frequently to give it the desired cross-section. *Opposite:* An old-fashioned blooming mill in operation.

Seamless-tube mill, National Tube Division, U.S. Steel Corporation, McKeesport, Pa. Seamless tubing is used, among other things, for water, gas and oil-drilling pipe; boiler tubing; cross-country pipelines for oil and natural gas; structural members on bicycles, and certain kinds of metal furniture.

Above: Piercing a billet to a make a seamless tube. The process begins when a solid steel bar (billet) is heated white-hot. It is then pierced by a mandrel and finished by being rolled in grooved rolls which reduces the wall thickness of the tube while simultaneously increasing its length. *Opposite:* Rolling structural steel.

Above: Coils of hot-rolled "strip" ready for shipment. *Opposite:*
Cold-reducing hot-rolled "strip" of steel plate.

Opposite: Tin plate inspection. *Above:* Wire mill. Wire is produced by rolling ingots into billets which in turn are rolled into rods from which the wire is drawn by pulling it through increasingly narrow dies.

Cable spinning begins by twisting wires in stranding machines,
then finishing the cable in a layer machine which revolves at great
speed while strands of wire are fed into the "twisting die." A
typical steel cable consists of seven smaller cables containing
19 wires each, a total of 133 wires.

Opposite: Drop forge, Wyman-Gordon Company, Harvey, Illinois. *Above:* Forging a crankshaft for a large diesel engine under a 20,000-pound "falling-weight double-action steam hammer" similar to the one shown on the opposite page.

Opposite: Forging automatic-pistol blanks at the Colt plant in Hartford, Conn. *Above:* After forging, small aircraft engine parts are hardened by being quenched in an oil bath.

People

Most people think of "industrial photography" as pictures of machinery in an atmosphere of fire and smoke. They are likely to forget that most pieces of machinery are operated by people—especially in the days before automation and computerization eliminated thousands of jobs and decimated the work force of the manufacturing industry. That this was not always so is documented on the following pages by pictures taken between 1942 and 1950.

That so many of the workers depicted here are women is no accident. The photographs were taken in the days when most able-bodied men were in the army, the navy or the marines and women had taken over their jobs, their symbol being "Rosie the Riveter." That they proved to be just as capable as men was doubtless an important factor in starting the movement subsequently known as "Women's Lib." Once women had convinced not only their male counterparts but also themselves that they could do a job just as well as men, the entire labor picture changed and the world would never be the same again. The "male chauvinist pig" was rapidly becoming an endangered species whose ultimate demise no thinking person can regret.

Opposite: A young woman at Colt's in Hartford, Conn., ably operates a milling machine.

Seven women at Colt's Hartford plant and one from United Aircraft do their jobs with pride. While most of them continued to work seriously while being photographed, two couldn't resist the temptation to smile. *Overleaf:* Women "manning" the DuMont tele-

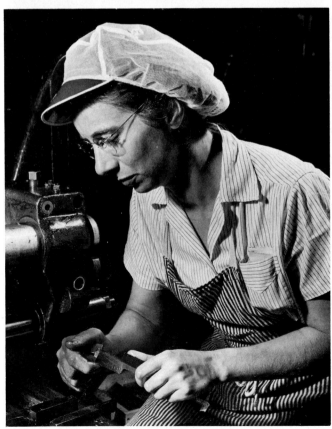

vision-receiver assembly line. About 150 workers were busy putting together the roughly 1,100 individual parts which were found in the average DuMont 21-inch TV set of 1950. At about every tenth place, an inspector checks the preceding group's work.

Above: A milling machine operator at the Colt plant in Hartford, Conn. *Opposite:* A drill-press operator at Pratt & Whitney's airplane-engine plant in Hartford, Conn. Both pictures were made in 1942.

Opposite: Men unload forged connecting-rod blanks at Pratt & Whitney's plant in Hartford, Conn. *Above:* Serial numbers are etched into finished airplane-engine cylinder sleeves.

Frequent careful inspection is one of the many vital requirements for any successful manufacturing process. Here, hawk-eyed inspectors at Pratt & Whitney's aircraft-engine plant in Hartford,

Conn., make sure that the respective engine parts—a crankshaft
and a connecting rod (which started as one of the blanks shown
on page 80) — will not fail in performance during operation.

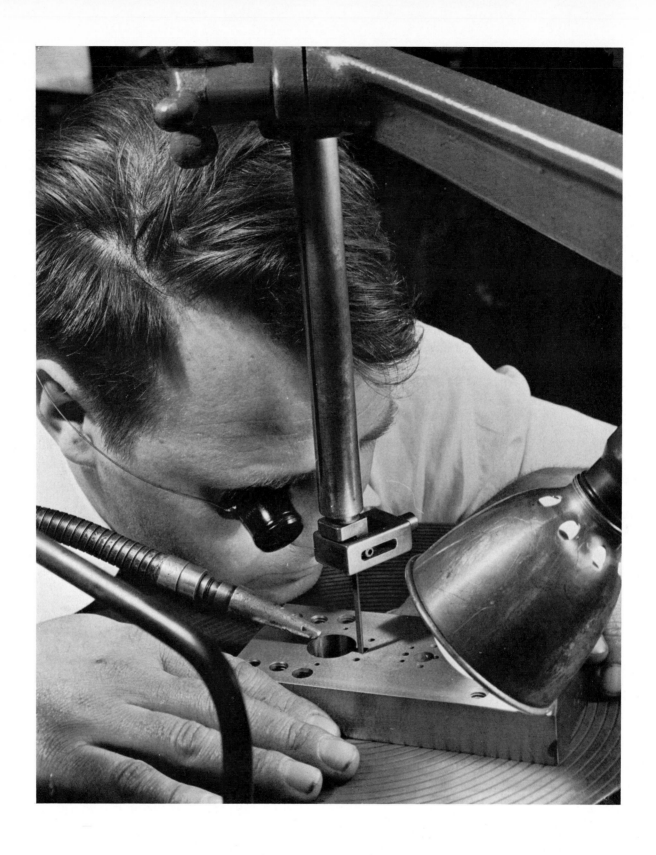

84

Above: A die maker works on a die which will be used to stamp out thousands of identical machine parts. Tolerances in die making are as critical as those applicable to fine Swiss watch movements. *Opposite:* Inspectors check airplane-engine parts.

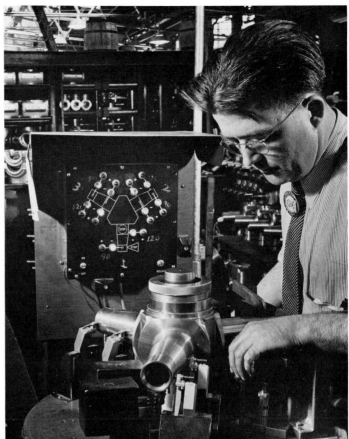

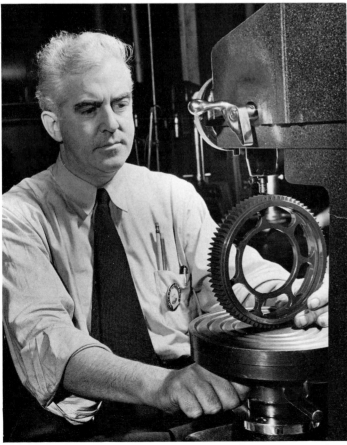

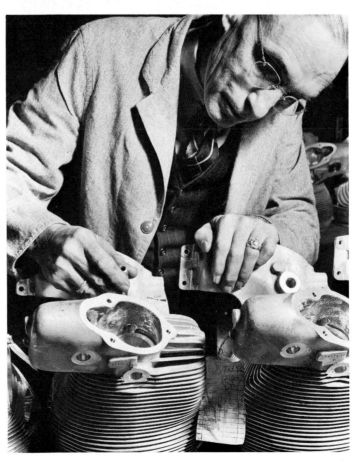

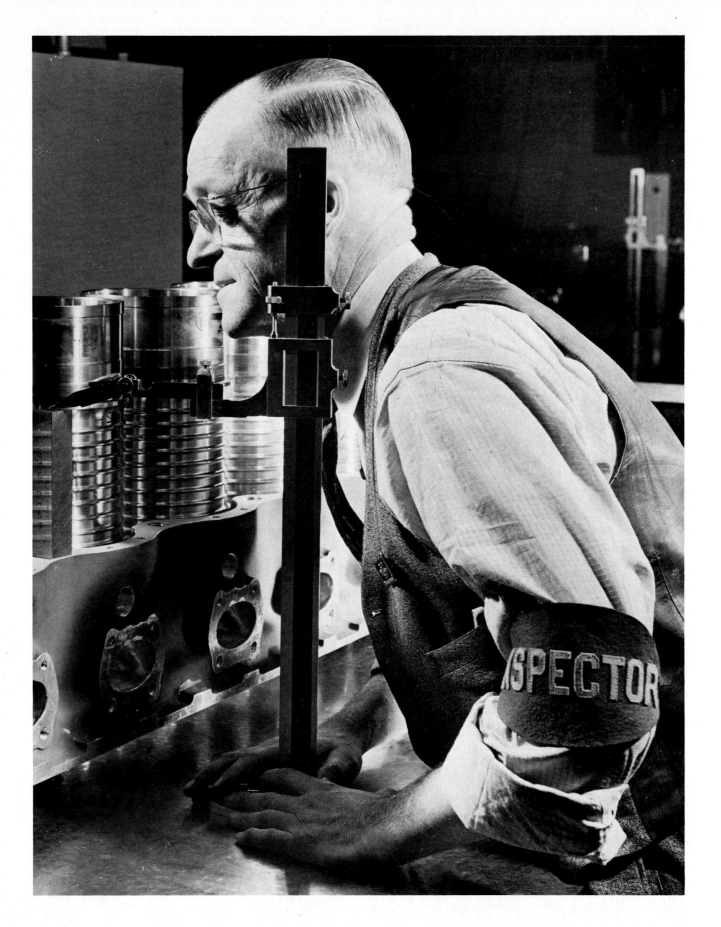

Inspectors check airplane cylinder sleeves and crankshafts.

Patterns in Industry

No photographer with an eye for aesthetic values can fail to notice the beauty inherent in many of the objects and operations he has to photograph. Time and again, in my industrial work, I found myself deviating from the straight and narrow path prescribed by "the script"— the picture editor's instruction sheets—to photograph subjects that were neither "listed" nor expected of me, simply because they were so beautiful, so "photogenic," so suitable to make the kind of photograph that attracts everybody's attention. And more often than not my instincts proved to be right and the respective picture was used in *Life,* often in full-page size.

In my experience, two principal characteristics are likely to make a photographic subject aesthetically attractive: clean-cut simplicity of line and form, and "patterns" based on repetition of similar or identical forms. The following pages contain such photographs—pictures which really don't "mean" much but which satisfy because of their "graphic" semiabstract beauty.

Opposite: A simple laboratory operation, insignificant in itself, makes an aesthetically satisfying picture merely because of its simplicity and arrangement in the form of a graphically attractive composition.

Industrial pattern shots. *Opposite:* Propeller axles for Allison fighter-plane engines. *Above:* Cylinder heads for radial aviation engines at Pratt & Whitney. *Below:* Hub cones at Hamilton Propeller works, Hartford, Conn.

Connecting rods for airplane engines ready for shipment. The exquisite quality of the workmanship defies description.

Castings for machine parts stacked in a warehouse. Repetition of
identical forms produces a pleasing pattern.

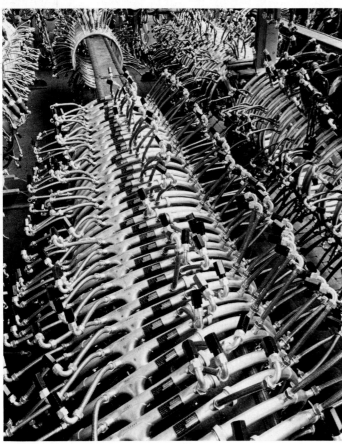

Opposite: Pattern shots of machine parts. *Above:* Test flight of a Coast Guard helicopter during the tryout of a newly developed light attached to the tips of the rotor blades. If successful, such lights might conceivably facilitate sea-air rescue operations at night. The ascending spiral design created by the whirling rotor lights results in an aesthetically satisfying picture. The white blob in the sky is the full moon, slightly distorted during the 2-minute time exposure required to make this shot.

95

War Production

From 1942 to 1946, in my capacity as an accredited, security-cleared war correspondent, I had a once-in-a-lifetime opportunity to visit, and photograph in, a great variety of different factories connected with our war effort, first on behalf of the Office of War Information (OWI) and later of *Life*. This proved to be a richly rewarding experience, giving me not only a chance to satisfy my interests in technical matters (I began my working life as an architect and structural engineer), but also offering me countless opportunities to use my special photographic knowledge and improve my phototechnical skills. Here is a partial listing of some of the places and operations I documented on film, examples of which are shown on the following pages:

A. O. Smith in Milwaukee, where I photographed aerial bomb production. Watervliet Arsenal near Schenectady, N.Y., where big guns are developed. The Colt small-arms factory in Hartford, Conn. Edgewood Arsenal, where the Army tests weapons connected with chemical warfare. The Autocar plant in Philadelphia, producer of four-wheel driven vehicles and half-tracks. The Chrysler Tank Arsenal in Detroit. The Sikorsky helicopter plant. The Consolidated Vultee plant in San Diego, Calif., a staging center for B-24 Liberator bombers. A B-36 bomber plant in the Southwest. The Curtiss-Wright Propeller Division in Caldwell, N.J. The Allison airplane-engine plant in Indianapolis, Ind. The Liberty Aircraft factory in Farmingdale, Long Island, N.Y. Rohm & Haas, makers of Plexiglas airplane nose cones and canopies. The Pratt & Whitney airplane engine-plant in East Hartford, Conn. LST's (Landing Ship, Tank) under construction in various shipyards. The building of cargo ships at the Federal Shipyard in Kearny, N.J. Ships' propeller manufacture at Bethlehem Steel Company's Richmond, Staten Island, plant. The American Locomotive Company in Schenectady, N.Y. A tire factory in Akron, O. Glass manufacture at different plants. And the manufacture of watch-movement jewels from synthetic rubies by Bulova.

Altogether, this collection of photographs, illustrating the working of American industry under wartime conditions, represents a historical document which may be unique because it was assembled not only by a specialist in industrial photography, but also by a photographer whose main concern was to produce images that are equally satisfying from the technical and the graphic-aesthetic point of view.

Opposite: A. O. Smith, Milwaukee. Cases for 500-pound aerial bombs ride on a fork lift.

98

Above: Forging 1,000-pound "blockbuster" bomb cases at A. O. Smith. *Opposite:* 500-pound aerial bomb cases ride an A. O. Smith conveyer line, their seemingly endless descent graphically symbolizing the endless stream of bombs that was required to crush Hitler's war machine.

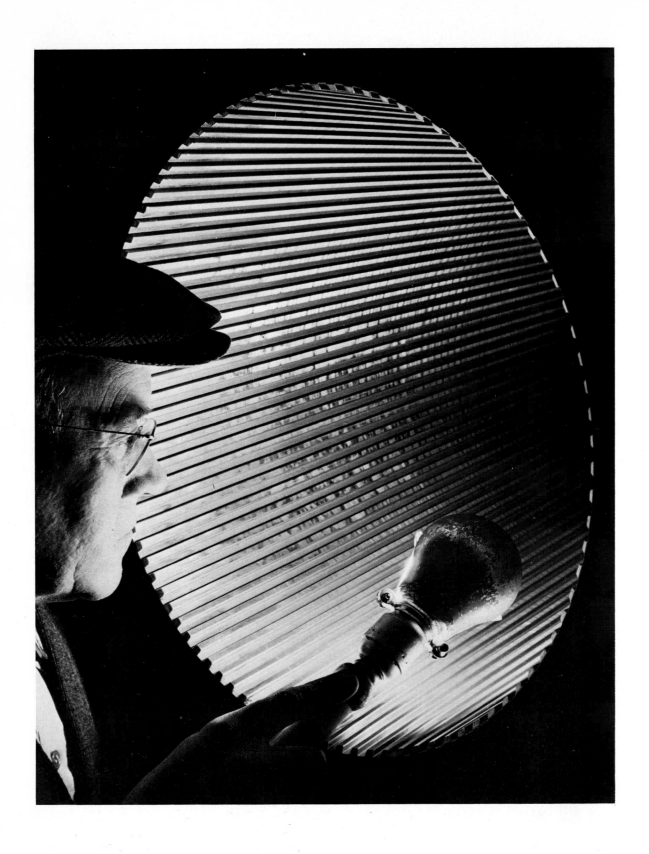

Watervliet Arsenal near Schenectady, N.Y. *Above:* Inspecting the barrel of a 16-inch naval gun of the kind that provided the main armament of American battleships of the Forties. *Opposite:* A view of the inside of the barrel of such a gun.

The gun shop at Watervliet Arsenal, N.Y. At the time these pictures were taken, the Arsenal, founded in 1813, was primarily concerned wtih research, development, engineering and pilot manufacturing of all types of cannons, up to and including the famous 280-mm atomic gun.

Above: Machine-gun barrels are turned on lathes at Colt's small-arms plant in Hartford, Conn. *Opposite:* A step in the manufacture of automatic pistols at Colt.

Above: Mortar shells loaded with Napalm are fired at an army test center. *Opposite:* Explosion of a Napalm mortar shell and the resulting rain of inextinguishable fire.

Above: A step in the manufacture of shells loaded with poisonous chemicals. Workers wear protective rubber coats and plastic face masks. *Opposite:* Testing the latest (1944) model of flamethrower.

110

Above: Four-wheel driven scout cars come off the assembly line of Autocar, Philadelphia. *Opposite:* The body of an Autocar armored half-track vehicle is lowered onto its chassis.

Workers weld inside the gun turrets at the Chrysler Tank Arsenal, Detroit, Mich. The blinding light from their torches together with the ink-black shadows make the scene appear like a preview of hell—or battle.

112

114

The tank assembly line at the Chrysler Tank Arsenal, Detroit, Mich., 1944. Finished tanks are lifted by overhead crane onto flatbed railroad cars to be shipped to the nearest port of embarkation for transport to the battlefields of Europe.

Aircraft, Ships, Locomotives...

The sinews of war are manifold, including virtually every industrially produced commodity from giant airplanes and battleships down to the almost invisibly small jewel bearings of gyroscopes used inside bombsights or the printing machinery pressed into the service of patriotic propaganda.

While making this kind of photograph, I was struck again and again by two things:

First, the incredible care lavished upon the production of means of destruction. Money, obviously, was no object, and the quality of workmanship surpassed by far anything ever expended on civilian goods. Typical examples are the airplane-engine connecting rods already shown on pages 83 and 92 and the Allison crankshaft seen on page 125, where every surface is not only machined but also polished until it shines like a mirror—something unheard of in, say, commercial automobile manufacture.

And secondly, the thought occurred to me, not once but countless times, that a large percentage of these so carefully produced goods would never reach their destination (and destiny) because too many ships were sunk by submarines, or, if they arrived safely, would be destroyed, perhaps within days and even hours. What a frightful waste, what an insane idea the entire concept of war! Just think how much good could be accomplished if the billions spent on war preparations (euphemistically called "defense") could be allotted to more worthy causes . . . such as education of highest quality for *everyone* (and let's not forget that everybody is a potential voter), pollution control, or family planning and birth control on a global scale. And I thought that the insanity of the Forties—the era of "conventional" weapons and explosives—was only child's play compared to the thinking of the politicians and military planners of the Eighties, the era of intercontinental missiles armed with multiple atomic warheads. And I asked myself: does humanity have enough time left to stop thinking in terms of "enemies" and start thinking of "human beings"? Because the only alternative to living together in peace (if not necessarily in harmony) on this finite earth is vanishing together in the fireball of a worldwide atomic blast.

Opposite: Sikorsky helicopters at the factory.

Above & opposite: B-24 Liberator bombers are checked out under camouflage netting outside the Consolidated Vultee plant in San Diego, Calif.

Overleaf: B-36 bombers under construction. Each of these giant bombers had eight engines: four jet engines and four piston-and-propeller engines.

Opposite: Finished propeller hubs on a conveyer at the Curtiss-Wright Propeller Division, Caldwell, N.J. *Above:* Propeller-hub inspector at work at Curtiss-Wright.

Opposite: Airplane engine assembly at Allison, Indianapolis, Ind.
Above: Crankshaft assembly at Allison. As much as possible, heavy metal is cut away to lighten airplane engines. Here, unnecessary metal has been drilled out of the crankshaft and a worker is plugging the holes with hollow light aluminum plugs.

125

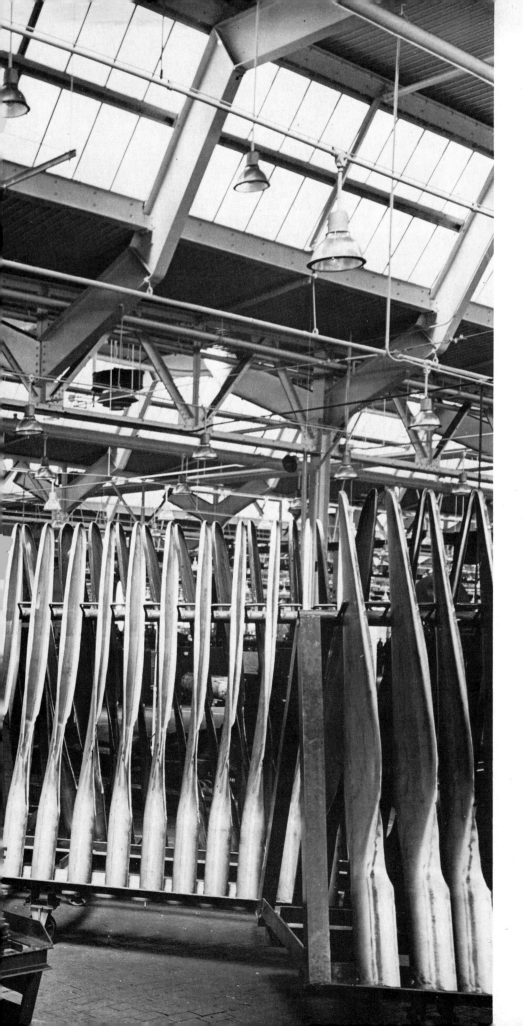

Forming propeller blades at Curtiss-Wright Corporation, Clifton, N.J. A partially formed propeller blade is carried away from a Birdsboro press. The 2,000-ton press shaped the sheets of premachined steel which can be seen lying on the skid in the foreground. Two pieces were subsequently welded together to form a hollow steel blade.

Finished three-blade propellers at the Curtiss-Wright Propeller Division in Clifton, N.J.

In the workshops at Liberty Aircraft Corp., Farmingdale, Long Island, N.Y., final inspection of tail assemblages is made before they are covered with fabric.

Women workers at Liberty Aircraft cover rudders and stabilizers
with cloth.

Above: At the Rohm & Haas Company, Bristol, Pa., a Plexiglas helicopter canopy is lifted out of the vacuum pot in which a heated and thereby softened sheet of Plexiglas was formed through applied pressure-differential by a technique called "free vacuum forming." *Opposite:* Plexiglas nose sections for Sikorsky R-5 helicopters are finished at Rohm & Haas.

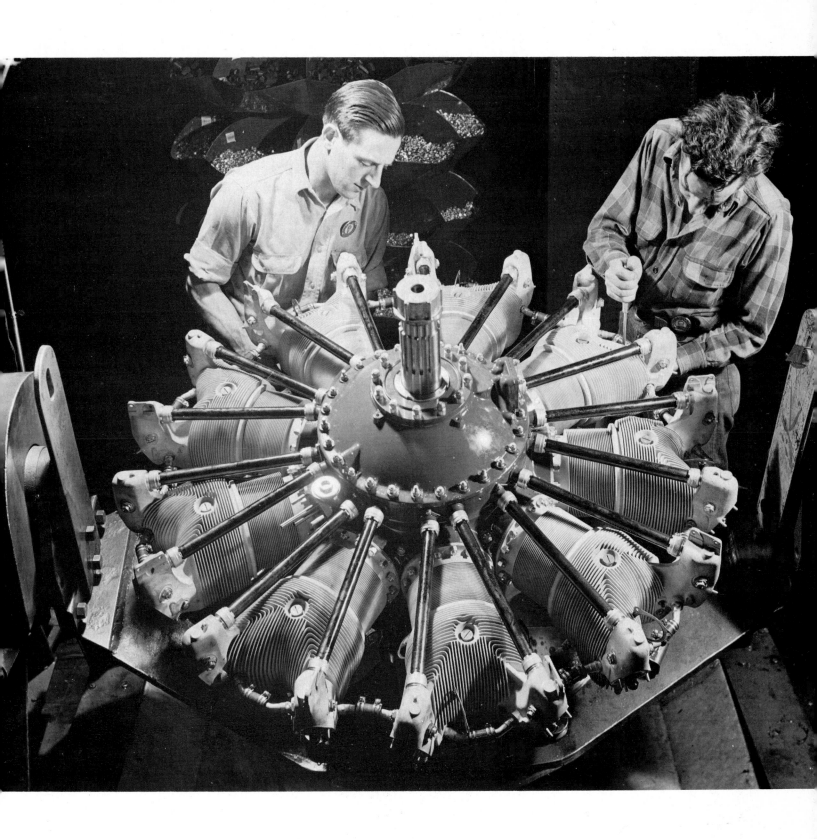

Opposite: A worker is mounting the pitch-control unit on a three-blade variable-pitch propeller at Curtiss-Wright. *Above:* Final assembly of an air-cooled radial 9-cylinder airplane engine.

Airplane engines on the test stand. A brand-new Allison in-line (*above*) and a 9-cylin-
der air-cooled Pratt & Whitney (*opposite*), each mounted in a test cell, roar their way

through their "green run," or first tryout. After completion of the run, each engine
will be completely dismantled and inspected piece by piece for possible flaws.

Blimp hangar under construction, Lakehurst, N.J. This huge structure was made entirely of wood held together with steel bolts.
Walking the narrow beams during construction took courage and
a fine sense of balance.

Above: An LST (Landing Ship, Tank) under construction at an East Coast shipyard. The ramp, on which the tanks will roll ashore, is being installed. *Opposite:* The battleship *Missouri* in dry dock at the Brooklyn Navy Yard, N.Y.

Above: Federal Shipyard, Kearny, N.J. The vessel is a C-3 type freighter of the *African Star* class, built for the Farrell Line and operated in its South African service. It is shown here in the final stage of construction, with hull complete, engines installed, super-structure nearly completed, and almost all king posts (vertical masts), to which cargo handling equipment is attached, erected. *Opposite:* Welders at work inside the hull of a Liberty cargo ship.

Opposite: Overall view of the propeller shop, Bethlehem Steel Company, Richmond, Staten Island, N.Y. *Above:* The pattern shop at Bethlehem Steel. Propeller patterns are usually constructed of kiln-dried pinewood segments, glued together, accurately finished to design, with shrinkage allowance to suit the propeller metal as required for the casting. The pattern normally consists of one blade attached to a segment of the hub. By revolving this pattern in a mold, three-, four-, five- and six-bladed propellers can be formed with the certainty that each blade will have exactly the same dimensions. Ships' propellers of this kind range from 5 to more than 22 feet in diameter and from 500 to 75,000 pounds in weight when finished.

Above: Finishing the mold at the propeller shop, Bethlehem Steel Company. To make this mold, a special kind of sand was formed around the wooden pattern shown in the preceding photograph. After the pattern is removed, all casting surfaces are sprayed with a mixture of graphite and molasses to bind the sand and assure a smooth casting. After closure (see the two following pages), pouring of the molten metal will begin. *Opposite:* The foundry at

Bethlehem Steel. Workmen have just completed pouring molten manganese bronze from the ladle visible in the upper left-hand corner. Depending on its size, the casting will stay in the mold from 48 to 96 hours for controlled cooling. The sand will then be removed and the casting allowed to cool for an additional 24 hours, as is the case with the propeller visible in the foreground.

The different parts of the completed mold are assembled at the
Bethlehem Steel propeller shop. Resemblance to certain works of

modern abstract sculpture is striking; these industrial forms have a
compelling beauty of their own.

150

These two photographs of the steam-locomotive assembly of the American Locomotive Company, Schenectady, N.Y. show a number of consolidation-type steamers under construction. Approxi-

mately 350 were built by ALCO during the war for the War
Department and were used by the U.S. and its allies overseas.

A turbine locomotive of the Pennsylvania Railroad. When this giant was built by the Baldwin Locomotive Works in 1945, it embodied completely new principles of locomotive design, but was obsolete only seven years later and is no longer in use. It covered 123 feet of track and weighed approximately 500 tons. Its

tender carried 37½ tons of coal, sufficient to drive the engine 220 miles. In the interest of the most effective pictorial rendition, I had the locomotive driven onto a turntable and turned until the sun illuminated it from what I considered the best possible direction.

Above: The turbine locomotive rounds a bend during a trial run.
Opposite: Railroad tracks in Nebraska, an arrow-straight road pointed at infinity.

The "500," passenger locomotive of the Chesapeake and Ohio Railway Company. This 154-foot-long engine, built jointly by the Baldwin Locomotive Works and the Westinghouse Electric Corporation and completed in 1948, incorporated radically new principles of construction: coal from the 29-ton bunker in the nose of the locomotive was conveyer-fed into the firebox (located behind

the cab) where a forced draft drove the flames through water-jacketed tubes, producing steam. The steam was used to operate generators that produced electric current to run the eight electric motors, which worked directly on the drive wheels of the locomotive. This engine, too, no longer exists.

Tire manufacture, Akron, Ohio.

Glassblowers at Corning Glass Works, Corn-ing, N.Y., blow blueprint machine cylin-ders. Glassblowing is a craft that is still es-sential to the glass industry, since only the glassblower can produce the precision glass-ware used in laboratories and delicate table glass. As a matter of fact, in 2,000 years, the art of glassblowing has hardly changed. The blowpipe, a hollow iron tube with a mouth-piece at one end and a small bulging knob at the other, is dipped into the molten glass by a workman called a "gatherer," and is lifted out with a "gather" of glass attached to the knob. The pipe is passed to a "ball holder" who, through carefully twirling the pipe and blowing through the mouthpiece, brings the molten glass to its first hollow form. The "coverer" then adds more glass to the first form, reshaping it and handing it to the "gaffer," the glassblowing team's most important member, who blows the glass to its final shape. Finally, a "crack-off boy" takes it away to let the glass cool off. After cooling, the piece of blown glassware is "cracked off" the pipe and finished.

Mirror for 200" Telescope
LARGEST PIECE OF GLASS
IN THE WORLD
WEIGHT 20 Tons
CAST 3-25-34 BY
CORNING GLASS WORKS

Opposite: The first of two 200-inch telescope mirrors, in 1934 the largest piece of glass in the world. Since it developed a crack during cooling, it could not be used and is now on exhibit in the Corning Museum of Glass. The second mirror forms the heart of the Hale telescope of the Mt. Palomar Observatory in California.
Above: A demonstration illustrates the fact that a certain kind of Corning dinnerware is virtually unbreakable.

Opposite: Flat glass emerges from the furnace at the Pittsburgh
Plate Glass Company. *Above:* A sheet of rough plate glass is lifted
off the conveyer preparatory to grinding and polishing.

Plate glass polishing line.

Checking plate glass for flaws.

Corning Glass Works, Corning, N.Y. Two steps in the manufacture of glass cloth of the kind used primarily for fireproof curtains. The almost microscopically fine strands of glass are woven very

much like animal or vegetable fibers. Their extreme thinness makes them highly flexible and virtually (but not quite) unbreakable—a quality one normally does not associate with glass.

171

Opposite: Stacks of glass tubing in a warehouse. *Above:* Fiberglass to be used for insulation emerges from a processing machine.

Opposite: A look into the miniature electric furnace of the Bulova Watch Company, Long Island City, N.Y., in which synthetic ruby crystals are "grown." Chemically indistinguishable from natural rubies, these crystals provide the raw material for the jewels in fine watch movements and other precision instruments. *Above:* Splitting a ruby boule prior to cutting it into the slices from which fine watch bearings are made.

A finished Bulova watch bearing made of synthetic ruby magnified 12 times.

A vial full of "jewels"—bearings intended for use in fine watch movements—seen four times natural size.

Above: A typesetter sets display type by hand with the aid of a "stick." *Opposite:* Linotype machines of the kind used by newspapers around 1940.

Above: The camera department of the Sterling Photo-Engraving Company, New York, N.Y., photographed in 1940. *Opposite:* Electrotyping; the acid bath. Electrotypes are made by using wax or plastic on the original type to make a mold on which copper is deposited by electrolysis. The copper shell is then backed up with lead to give it stability. In printing, such electrotypes can be flat for use on flatbed presses or curved for rotary presses.

Opposite: A flatbed press is made ready for printing. *Above:* A five-color rotary press photographed in 1940 at the Arrow Press, New York, N.Y. Curved electrotype page plates are being attached to the cylinders by pressmen. These plates must be positioned with extreme accuracy so that the design on one cylinder will register exactly with the design on all the others. Ink of a different color is then applied to each plate cylinder. In this way, by proper combination of the colors blue, red, yellow and black (the fifth color is not always used), any imaginable shade of color can be produced.

When I photographed the radio telescope at Greenbank, W. Va. in 1960, it was being used to scan the void for signs of extraterrestrial intelligence. The streaks in the sky were traced by stars, which moved during the 15-minute time exposure.